To Praise, To Bless, To Preach

Art by Maurice Keating OP

Text by Dominican Laity Brisbane

Dominican Series

The Dominican Series is a joint project by Australian Dominican women and men and offers contributions on topics of Dominican interest and various aspects of church, theology and religion in the world.

Series Editors: Mark O'Brien OP and Gabrielle Kelly OP

1. *English for Theology: A Resource for Teachers and Students*, Gabrielle Kelly OP, 2004.
2. *Towards the Intelligent Use of Liberty: Dominican Approaches in Education,* edited by Gabrielle Kelly OP and Kevin Saunders OP, 2007.
3. *Preaching Justice: Dominican Contributions to Social Ethics in the Twentieth Century,* edited by Francesco Campagnoni OP and Helen Alford OP, 2008.
4. *Don't Put Out The Burning Bush: Worship and preaching in a Complex World,* edited by Vivian Boland, 2008.
5. *Bible Dictionary: Selected Biblical and Theological Words,* Gabrielle Kelly OP in collaboration with Joy Sandefur, 2008.
6. *Sunday Matters A: Reflections on the Lectionary Readings for Year A,* Mark O'Brien OP, 2010.
7. *Sunday Matters B: Reflections on the Lectionary Readings for Year B,* Mark O'Brien OP, 2011.
8. *Sunday Matters C: Reflections on the Lectionary Readings for Year C,* Mark O'Brien OP, 2012.
9. *Scanning the Signs of the Times: French Dominicans in the Twentieth Century,* Thomas F O'Meara OP and Paul Philibert OP, 2013.
10. *From North to South: Southern Scholars Engage with Edward Schillebeeckx,* edited by Helen F Bergin OP, 2013.
11. *Thee ABC of Sunday Matters,* Mark O'Brien OP, 2013.
12. *Restoring the Right Relationship: The Bible on Divine Righteousness,* Mark O'Brien OP, 2014.
13. *Dominicans and Human Rights,* Mark Deeb OP and Celestina Veloso Freitas OP, 2017.
14. *The Promise of Renewal: Dominicans and Vatican II,* Mike Attridge, Daren Dias OP, Matthew Eaton, Nicolas Olkovich

ISBN: 978-1-925643-52-7 (paperback)
978-1-925643-53-4 (hardback)
978-1-925643-54-1 (epub)
978-1-925643-55-8 (pdf)

Published by:

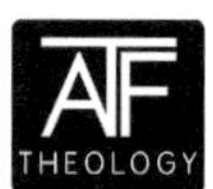

An imprint of the ATF Press Publishing
Group owned by ATF (Australia) Ltd.
PO Box 504
Hindmarsh, SA 5007
ABN 90 116 359 963
www.atfpress.com
Making a lasting impact

To Praise, To Bless, To Preach

A Dominican Artistic Appreciation of 800 Years of Divine Grace

Art by Maurice Keating OP

Text by Dominican Laity Brisbane

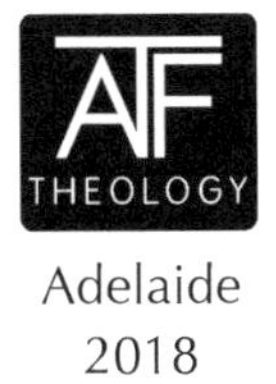

Adelaide
2018

Table of Contents

Foreword

Fr Maurice Keating's Artwork

My first introduction to the Art of Fr Maurice Keating was when I entered the Dominican novitiate at St Dominic's, Melbourne in early 1966. In the novitiate corridor there were a set of stations of the cross where the spectral figures were drawn in white or red crayon over a very black crayon background. They were a stark and powerful set of stations, full of suffering. Years later I saw a similar set by Fr Maurice in the chapel of the Dominican house at Bomana in Papua New Guinea. Here however the background was white and the still spectral figures were in black or red. Here the stations were not quite so sombre, but still had a strong impact.

In between those two sets of stations of the cross I have seen quite a lot of Fr. Maurice's artwork. One item I remember well was a Calvary scene which hung in one of the common rooms in the Blackfriars Retreat Centre at Watson, ACT. It was painted in a sort of cubist style with sharp angles in the stark semi-desert landscape with the three crosses in the distance. It was a large painting and it must have had a notable impact on at least one couple who were at Blackfriars for a retreat or a marriage encounter program. They liked it so much that they made Fr Maurice an offer for the painting which he could not refuse, so he told me, and so it went off to grace their lounge room or some other part of their home.

Some of Fr Maurice's best work has been his mosaics. He was painstaking in his collection of broken pieces of coloured tiles which he was then able to use to give the timeless effect of mozaics of the risen Christ, the Blessed Virgin and the saints. As might be expected, there is a very fine mosaic of the Blessed Virgin Mary giving the rosary to St Dominic in the Dominican Church of Our Lady of the Rosary at

Watson in Canberra, where Fr Maurice lived and worked for many years. In the same church the stations of the cross are impressive with stark figures in black against a background of lighter coloured mosaic. Some of his best work in this medium is to be seen in the Church of St Joseph at O'Connor in the ACT. He also made some fine mosaic coats of arms for our university colleges. St Albert's College at the University of New England, Armidale, NSW, and John XXIII College at the Australian National University in Canberra are two which spring to mind.

Fr Maurice has always painted Dominican Saints, and a fine painting of St Thomas Aquinas is in Rosary Church at Watson. Of more recent times while based at St Martin's Priory in Brisbane Fr Maurice has been painting some lesser-known Dominican Saints and Blesseds. He has in the last few years completed a series of House patrons for Blackfriars Priory School in Adelaide, all of whom were Dominicans but not all being saints or blesseds. More recently he has completed a series of paintings on Dominican themes and Dominican Saints for San Sisto College at Carina in Brisbane, opposite the Priory.

In his over fifty years in the Dominican Order Fr Maurice has been very prolific in his production of art, especially with Dominican themes. He has used various mediums in his artwork over the years, and whether based in Canberra, the Solomon Islands, Bomana in Papua New Guinea or in Brisbane he has always been productive and sought to respond where he saw a need for religious art to mediate a spiritual reality to those seeking an insight into the eternal.

Fr. Kevin Saunders, OP,
Provincial
August 2016

Introduction

When Fr Tom Cassidy OP, as the Prior of Our Lady of Graces Parish, Carina, asked the local chapter of Lay Dominicans whether there was interest in writing brief biographies of some saintly Dominicans to accompany the art works of Fr Maurice Keating OP, the Lay Dominicans unanimously agreed. They were well aware that among the priory's Dominican priests, indeed acting as their Lay Dominican chaplain, was an artist with a natural talent. Furthermore it was already 2016 with the mood of the Dominican octocentenary in the air, and the book to emerge would commemorate this anniversary.

Early in the thirteenth century, St Dominic de Guzman showed a zeal for correcting heresy and spreading *truth* that could bring people into God's kingdom. 'Truth' has remained an essential element of the Dominican Order and remains one of three significant mottos of the Order. Dominic spent many hours in quiet prayer, and it was said that he spoke only to God and about God. Fittingly two other principal mottos of the Order are 'To contemplate and hand on to others the fruits of contemplation' and 'To praise, to bless, to preach'. These three mottos are clearly interrelated and are reflected in the lives of the Dominican Saints and Blesseds.

The Dominicans and those associated with the Order have cause to celebrate not only the Order's endurance, extensiveness and the numbers of blessed and canonized, but also the very charism of preaching. This charism was the particular reason for the Order's foundation at a time when there was strong reluctance to authorise more religious Orders. The Dominican charism with its implications for daily life is inspiringly and succinctly expressed by the Dominican Sisters of Eastern Australia and the Solomon Islands: 'Dominicans are called by the Spirit to be faithful to the prophetic mission of Jesus by the integrity of our lives, and to proclaim the truth fearlessly and confidently, as Dominic did.'[1]

Papal approval for the Dominican Order or the 'Order of Preachers' was granted by Pope Honorius III on 22 December 1216. On the occasion of the its 800th anniversary in 2016, the Dominican Order has members in more than 110 countries and includes priests, brothers, sisters, cloistered nuns, and Lay Dominicans (formerly Third Order or Tertiaries.) There are also associated groups such as the Confraternity of the Rosary. There have been over seventy Dominican saints and over 200 blesseds through the centuries since the Order's official papal recognition in 1216.

The sparks of God's light and God's grace which have shone into the world through Dominican achievements since 1216 indeed warrant celebration. Recognising God as the source of faith and of every good thing, the Dominican Order is appropriately grateful and 'boasting' in God's goodness and the knowledge of it (Jeremiah 9:24).

This commemorative book glimpses how prayerful and devoted lives can radiate blessings to those around, in ways that sometimes must be explained as 'miraculous', but which are always rooted in love. As Cardinal Congar, OP wrote 'it is impossible, without love, to submit one's soul to another person, or to give oneself in spiritual service'.[2]

The book gives a glimpse of Saint Dominic and fifteen other blessed or canonised Dominicans who lived over the period until the twentieth century. Whether their major contributions were intellectual truths, spiritual truths, relief of hunger and physical discomfort, amelioration of social division, their own lives in martyrdom, or any kind of gift to the world, Saint Dominic and the fifteen featured Dominicans transmitted a flow of God's living energy in everyday situations, often where there was pain and suffering; and so in multifarious ways they led their contemporaries towards a greater awareness of God's nature and powerful presence.

---

1. Dominican Sisters of Eastern Australia and the Solomon Islands, Mission statement quoted in *Explore Our Charism* (www.opeast.org.au/explore-our-charism)
2. Yves Congar, 'St Thomas Aquinas: Servant of Truth', first published in *Faith and Spiritual Life*, translated by A Manson and LC Sheppard (New York: Herder and Herder, 1968), 67–85

This book, therefore, provides a glimpse and a memento of the overall contribution of the Dominican Order throughout the world. The book includes readily accessible images of Fr Maurice Keating's sketched portraits. A brief biography accompanies each sketch. In sketching these crayon portraits, Fr Maurice Keating has reproduced works by various artists over the centuries. His renderings seem to capture and convey the emotions and moods of these women and men caught up in the Dominican experience of God and service to God.

Fr Maurice Keating was born in Tasmania and since ordination has served in several Australasian parishes including the Solomon Islands. He presently serves at the Dominican parish of Our Lady of Graces in Carina, Brisbane. Fr Maurice is largely self-taught as an artist. Although he is a humble man who recoils from recognition and praise of his work, it seemed fitting to enjoy and celebrate his gift at a time when the many other Blessings of the Lord upon the Dominican Order over 800 years are also being celebrated.

While the book is intended primarily for those with experience of, or interest in, the Dominican Order, it is hoped that the book will also be of value more widely for increased appreciation of Saint Dominic, the Dominicans and their charism. It also serves as a reminder of the closeness of God and the availability of His Kingdom to all those who prayerfully seek God and God's will.

Dominican Laity
Brisbane
Australia

Saint Dominic de Guzman

'We are meant to sow the seed; not hoard it.'

St Dominic, the founder of the Order of Preachers, was born around 1170–1173 in Caleruega, Spain. After finishing his studies at Palencia, he was ordained a priest and became a Canon Regular at Osma. Dominic was a man of much prayer and contemplation.

He was selected by Bishop Diego of Osma to accompany him on diplomatic missions in 1203 and 1204. As they travelled through southern France, they were disappointed by encountering numerous followers of the Albigensian heresy, including former Christians. Inspired and with the Pope's approval, they began to preach against Albigensianism together with the Cistercians.

Dominic continued to preach while living in poverty. The Albigensians won admiration by living austerely, while priests and bishops often lived in comparative luxury, and sometimes laxity. Dominic, recognizing the value of self-denial and poverty, walked barefoot and begged.

His preaching yielded conversions and attracted followers. In 1206 he established a monastery for women in Prouille, France. The women of this community were officially recognized as nuns in 1215.

Dominic understood the benefits of sound education for preachers and teachers who would spread the truth of the gospel. This became a reality in Toulouse in 1215 when Dominic organized a new religious order near centres of learning. On 22 December 1216, Papal approval for the "Order of Preachers" was granted by Pope Honorius III. In 1217 Dominic disseminated his small group of preachers throughout Europe.

Numerous miracles including instant cures and returning the dead to life occurred through Saint Dominic. He died in Bologna on 6th August 1221, and was canonised in 1234. His Feast Day is celebrated on the 8th August except in Australia and New Zealand where it is celebrated on 3 August.

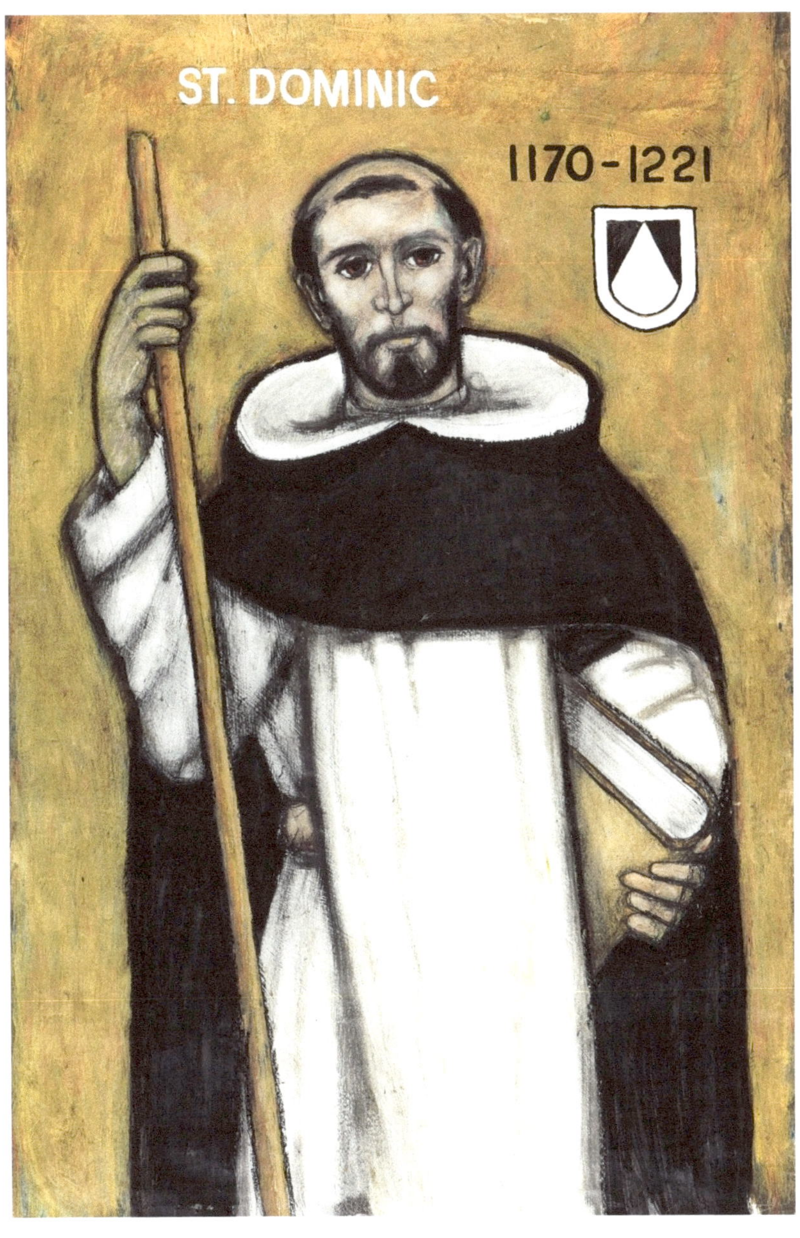
ST. DOMINIC
1170 - 1221

Saint Hyacinth

'For (poverty) is the testament or authentic instrument by which we claim eternal life.'

Saint Hyacinth, also known as the 'Apostle of the North' and the 'Apostle of Poland', was born in 1185 in Poland. Hyacinth met Saint Dominic in Rome in the last years of Dominic's life, and became a Dominican friar. He is said to have been greatly inspired by witnessing the miracle of a dead youth's return to life through Dominic's prayer. He returned to Poland where he established church communities and preached throughout Northern Europe, bringing conversion to many. He visited the sick in hospitals and used his own income to give financial assistance to the poor.

In Kiev, he crossed the surface of the deep River Dnieper in a miraculous manner when fleeing from the danger of the attacking Tartars. He is also known for numerous other miracles.

He became ill with a fever on St Dominic's Feast Day in 1257, and died on the Feast of the Assumption. He was canonised in 1594.

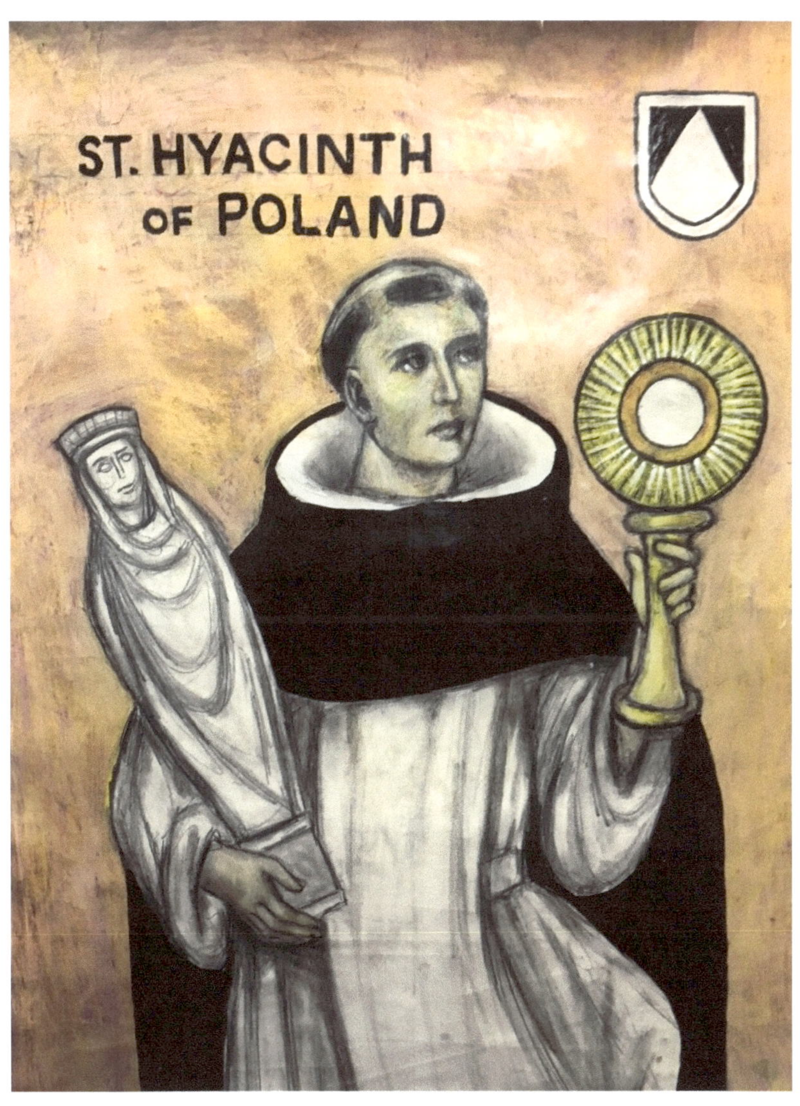
ST. HYACINTH
OF POLAND

Blessed Jordan of Saxony

Blessed Jordan of Saxony was born in Germany around 1190, reportedly of a noble family. Jordan completed studies and received his degree in Paris where he met St Dominic. He was inspired by the preaching of Blessed Reginald and became a Dominican in 1220. He was elected Prior Provincial of Lombardy the next year, and in 1222, St Dominic having died, Jordan was elected to succeed him as Master General of the Dominicans.

Some have said that mothers feared losing their sons and universities feared losing their best students to the Dominican Order through Jordan's powerful preaching and his attractive interpersonal manner. Certainly when he preached to young students at universities, he inspired and drew many to the Dominican Order including St Albert the Great. Jordan also acted as spiritual guide in the newly formed Order, and he expanded the Order, establishing new foundations in Germany and Switzerland, and sending missionaries to Denmark.

Blessed Jordan wrote an account of the life of St Dominic and the origins of the Order of Preachers. It remains a principal source of early Dominican information, being written as early as about 1233 and being of undisputed authorship.

Blessed Jordan died on his way from the Holy Land in late 1236 or early 1237 in a shipwreck off the coast of Syria in which none survived. His feast day is 15 February.

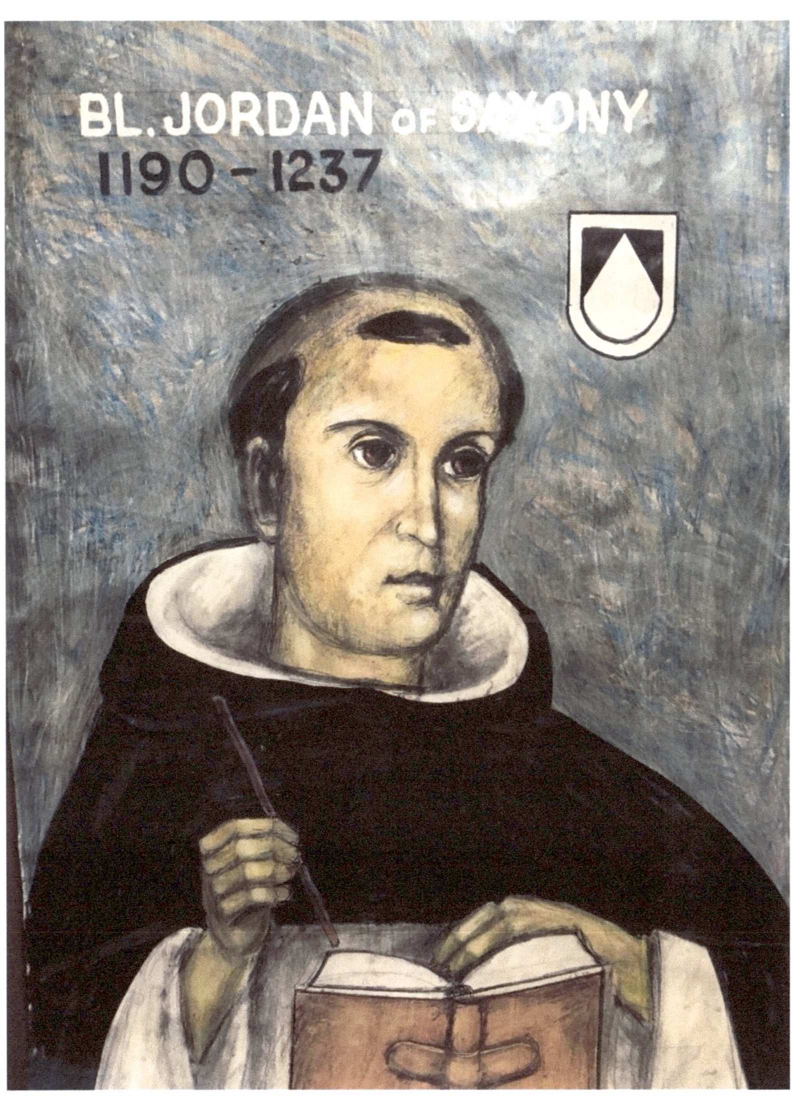
BL. JORDAN OF SAXONY
1190 - 1237

Saint Albert the Great

'If we possess charity then we possess God, for God is charity.'

Albert was born around 1200 in a region which is now a part of Germany. He studied at the University of Padua, perhaps also at Bologna, and the University of Paris which was then the intellectual centre of Western Europe. Albert joined the Dominican Order in about 1223 and was ordained about 1228. He became the first German Dominican friar to receive a Master of Theology degree and was appointed the Papal Theologian in Rome. Albert preached throughout the German and Bohemian regions, becoming one of the most famous preachers in Western Europe.

Albert was recognized as one of the great scholars of his times, being known as 'Albert the Great' ('Albertus Magnus') and 'Universal Doctor'. He was instrumental in bringing the writings of Aristotle to Western thought, and he pioneered the use of the inductive method of reasoning. Thomas Aquinas came under his influence as his pupil in Cologne.

Many of his writings focused on 'Mary, Mother of Jesus'. In addition to his theological and philosophical achievements, Albert was a renowned scholar and researcher in the natural sciences. He studied animals, birds, insects, plants and minerals. His forty volumes of writings served as an encyclopaedia of contemporary European knowledge as it included his works on astronomy, biology, chemistry, geography, mathematics, mineralogy, physics, philosophy, and theology.

Albert died in 1280 and was canonized in 1931. Pope Pius XII proclaimed him Patron Saint of Natural Scientists In 1941. His feast day is 15 November.

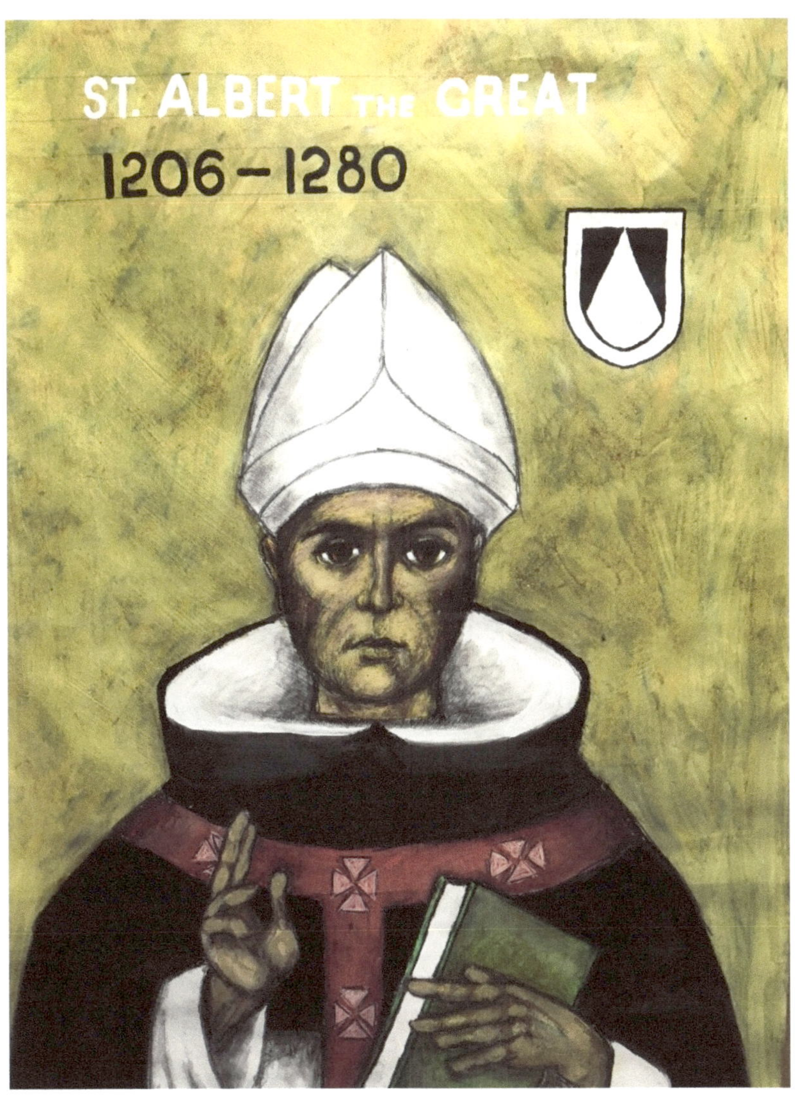
ST. ALBERT THE GREAT
1206 – 1280

Saint Peter Martyr (a.k.a. Saint Peter of Verona)

'God loves us beyond comprehension and we cannot diminish God's love for us.'

Saint Peter Martyr, also known as saint Peter of Verona, was born about 1205 in Verona, Northern Italy. His parents followed or sympathized with the Cathar heresy. He attended the University of Bologna and at the age of fifteen, he met Saint Dominic. Peter joined the Dominicans, and preached against the hypocrisy of expressions of faith that were not supported by actions.

From the 1230's, he also preached against heresy, particularly Catharism which was widely followed in northern Italy. He preached in Bologna, Como, Florence, Genoa and Rome. Crowds gathered to hear him and many were converted including Catharists who turned or returned to Orthodoxy. It is said that once, when his large audience was under the scorching sun while he preached, some heretics challenged him to provide shade, whereupon a cover of clouds appeared as he prayed.

In 1251, Pope Innocent IV appointed him Inquisitor of Lombardy. In this role, on 6 April 1252, he was attacked with an axe to the head. He stated the first article of the Apostles' Creed before dying. His assassin, named Carino, later repented, converted and became a Dominican lay brother known as Carino of Balsamo.

In March 1253, less than a year after his death, St Peter was canonized; this is said by some to be the fastest canonisation in papal history. Numerous miracles were attributed to him both in his earthly life and after it.

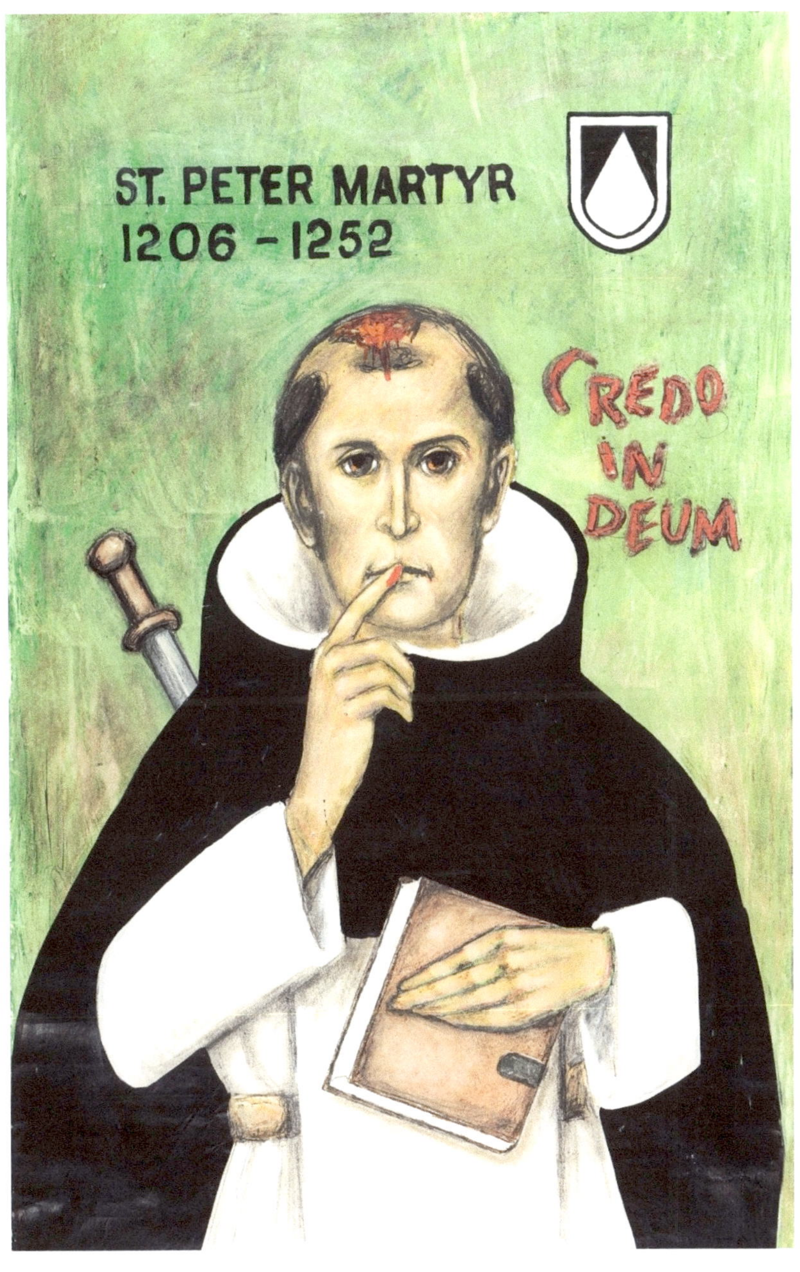
ST. PETER MARTYR
1206 - 1252
CREDO
IN
DEUM

Saint Thomas Aquinas

'To one who has faith no explanation is necessary.
To one without faith no explanation is possible.'

Thomas Aquinas was a priest, professor and philosopher who has significantly influenced religious and academic thought. He methodically harmonized faith and reason. His work is studied to this day with powerful effect. He is known as 'The Angelic Doctor'.

St. Thomas was born to nobility about 1225 in Roccasecca in Italy, and joined the Dominican Order between 1240 and 1244. His family objected and kept him in their family tower for about a year, before he undertook further studies in Paris and probably Cologne, and was ordained.

He taught in universities during the 'Scholastic Era', when the ancient logic of Aristotle was being revived. The Roman Catholic Church had some serious reservations about the Aristotelian school of thought. Thomas Aquinas reconciled the two by granting reason its own integrity. He used Aristotelian arguments to 'prove' the existence of God and the truth of Christian beliefs, while also maintaining that some doctrinal truths are revealed only through faith. He painstakingly question-and-answered his way through two major works: *Summa Contra Gentiles* and *Summa Theologica*.

His thinking, later called 'Thomism', was very quickly validated by the Roman Catholic Church. He wrote many other works and he remains one of the Church's most influential theological contributors. He was, however, a man of remarkable humility.

Thomas Aquinas died on 7th March 1274. He was canonized in 1323 and proclaimed 'Doctor of the church' in 1567. In 1879 Pope Leo XIII declared Aquinas's works 'the only true philosophy'. His feast day is 28 January.

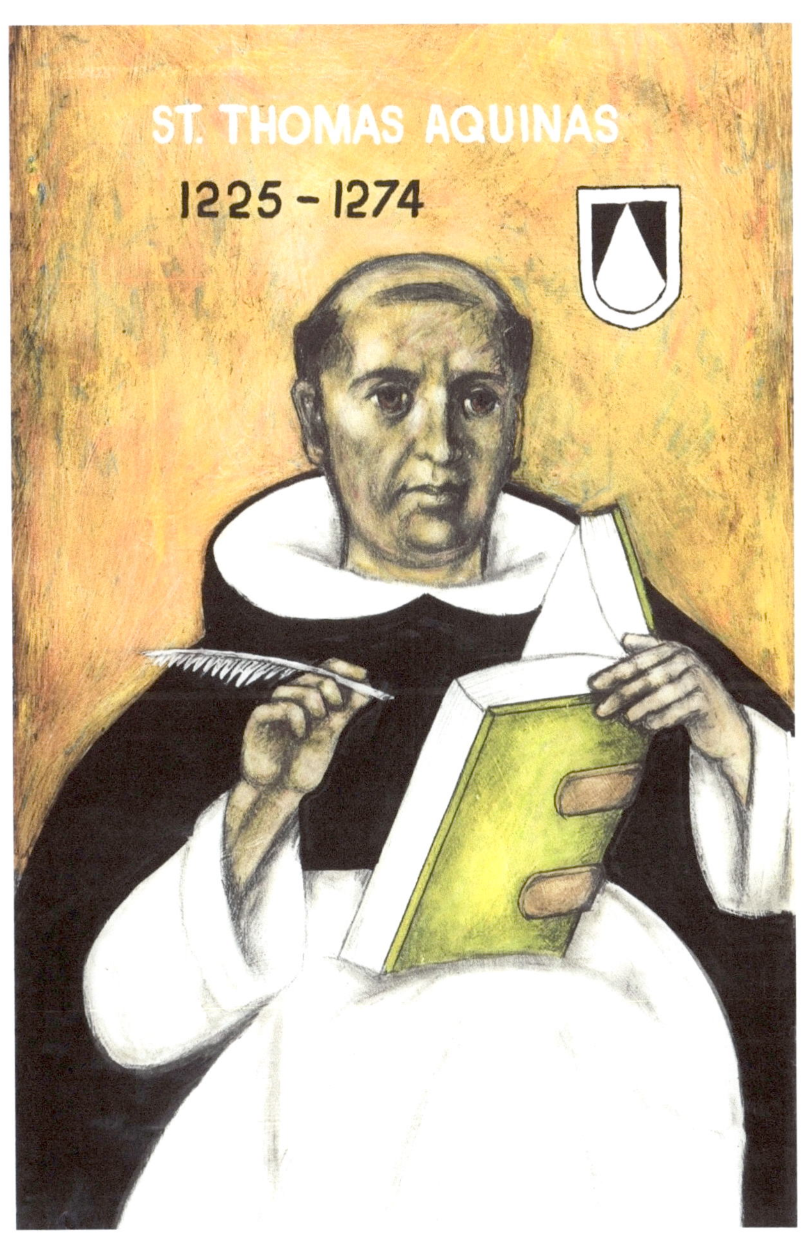
ST. THOMAS AQUINAS
1225 - 1274

Saint Margaret of Hungary

'I prefer to be among those who consider that they have no time to lose if they wish to give God all the glory that they can before they die.'

St Margaret of Hungary was born in the 18th January 1242 to King Bela IV of Hungary and Maria Lascaris who was the daughter of an emperor. Her parents are said to have vowed to dedicate their daughter to God if Hungary were liberated from the invading Tartars. The Tartars were defeated, and consequently when Margaret was three or four years old, her parents sent her to the Dominican Monastery of Veszprem. When she was about twelve years old, Margaret moved to a convent which was founded by her parents on an island in the Danube, now known as Margaret Island. There she made her profession in 1255.

Margaret resolutely resisted her father's attempts to arrange for her a marriage to King Ottokar II of Bohemia. Instead she took solemn vows in the Dominican Order when she was around eighteen years old.

From her early life, Margaret was notable for her extreme devotion, prayerfulness, self-denial, mortifications and humility. Regardless of her noble heritage, she undertook the most unpleasant and lowly tasks in helping the sick and in other convent work. Margaret had a special love for the Eucharist and the Passion of Christ Jesus. She was also devoted to the Holy Spirit and to Mary. Miraculous events are recorded as occurring in Saint Margaret's life and after.

She died in 1270 or 1271 and was canonized by Pope Pius XII in 1943. Her feast day is celebrated on the 18 January.

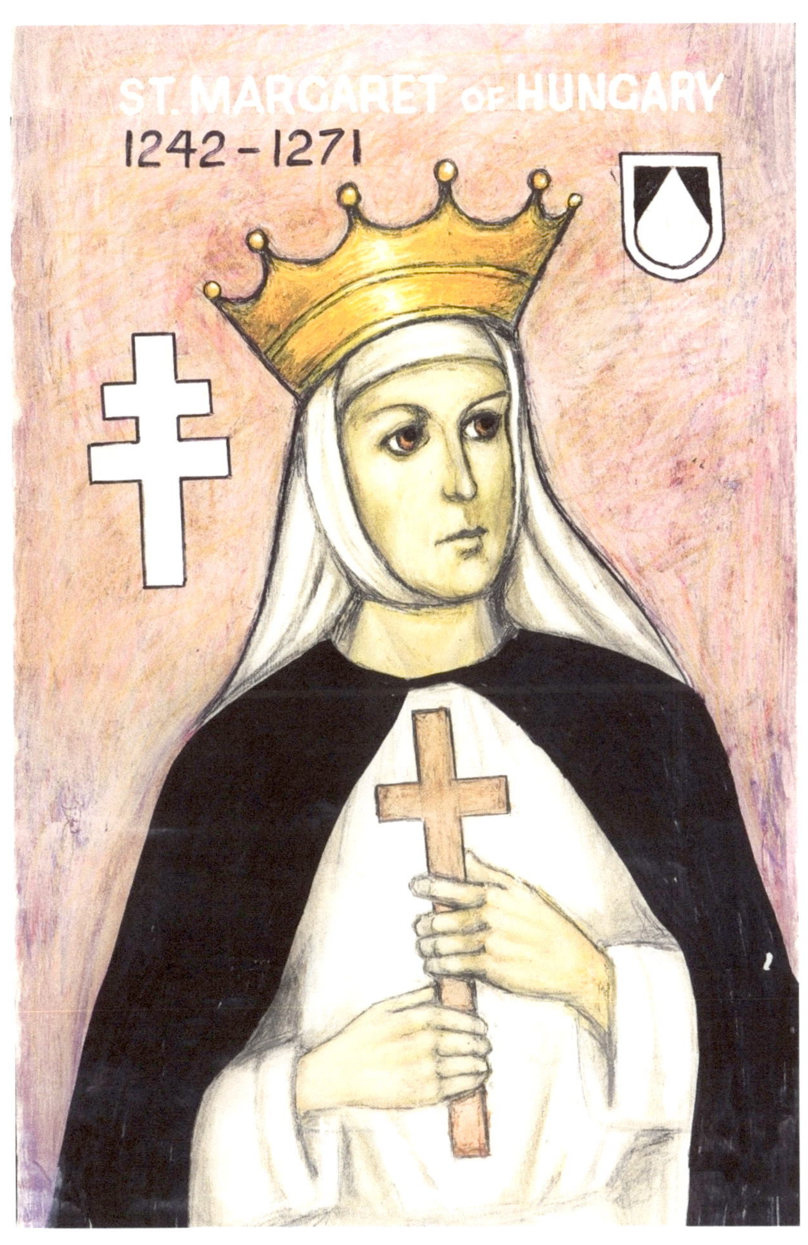
ST. MARGARET OF HUNGARY
1242-1271

Blessed Margaret of Castello

"If only you knew what I carried in my heart, you would marvel!"

In 1287 Blessed Margaret of Castello was born blind and suffered severe physical disabilities. She underwent prayer in the hope of healing, but her disabilities remained. Margaret was rejected by her parents, but people in the town of Castello recognized her spirituality and the cheerfulness which she spread despite her circumstances.

After spending some time with the Dominican nuns, she became a Dominican tertiary. She cared for children, the sick and dying. Also, by her prayer and example, she assisted prisoners, disharmonious families and people who had lost faith and despaired. Although Margaret was deprived of love and companionship from her parents, she showed God's love to the world.

Margaret died on the 13th April 1320, aged 33. It is recorded that a crippled child who touched her body was freed from her deformity, and more than 200 miracles have been attributed to her since then. Her body was witnessed to be perfectly preserved when exhumed in 1558, although examination indicated no chemicals had been used to aid preservation. The body remains incorrupt. She was beatified in 1609.

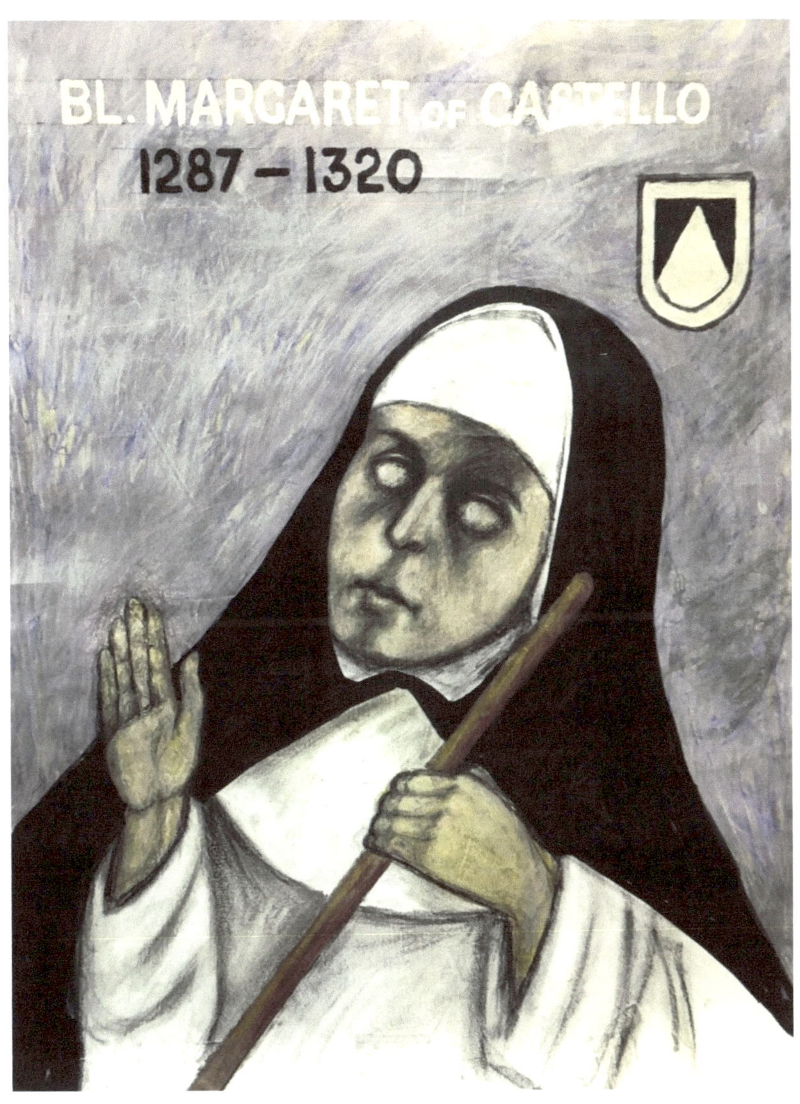
BL. MARGARET OF
1287 – 1320

Saint Catherine of Siena

'Be who God meant you to be and you will set the world on fire.'

Catherine was born in Siena in 1347. From the age of about six she started receiving visions, and then embarked on a life of devotion. She spent many hours praying alone and used severe mortification practices. Her devotion culminated in her receiving the stigmata, although hers remained invisible until after her death.

Her parents were intent on her marrying but relented, permitting her to join the Dominican Tertiary sisters (Dominican Laity) in 1363. Soon she started assisting in the local hospital. When dealing with those affected by plague, she was reported to exude joy and speak words that often elicited conversions, and also to heal many.

In 1374 Catherine started to travel and became very influential in political affairs. She worked with city officials in dissuading them from joining the Anti-Papal League. She represented Florence to Pope Gregory XI. She then advised Gregory XI to return to Rome and thus helped end the Avignon Papacy. Catherine also lobbied Gregory's successor, Urban VI, to bring an end to the subsequent schism. She worked towards these outcomes both in personal meetings and through her letters, being a prolific letter writer. Other writings of hers included mystical and devotional literature.

Catherine died in 1380 and was canonized in 1461. In 1939 she was named patron saint of Italy, alongside St Francis. In 1970 she was proclaimed Doctor of the Church. John Paul II named her one of six patron saints of Europe in 1999.

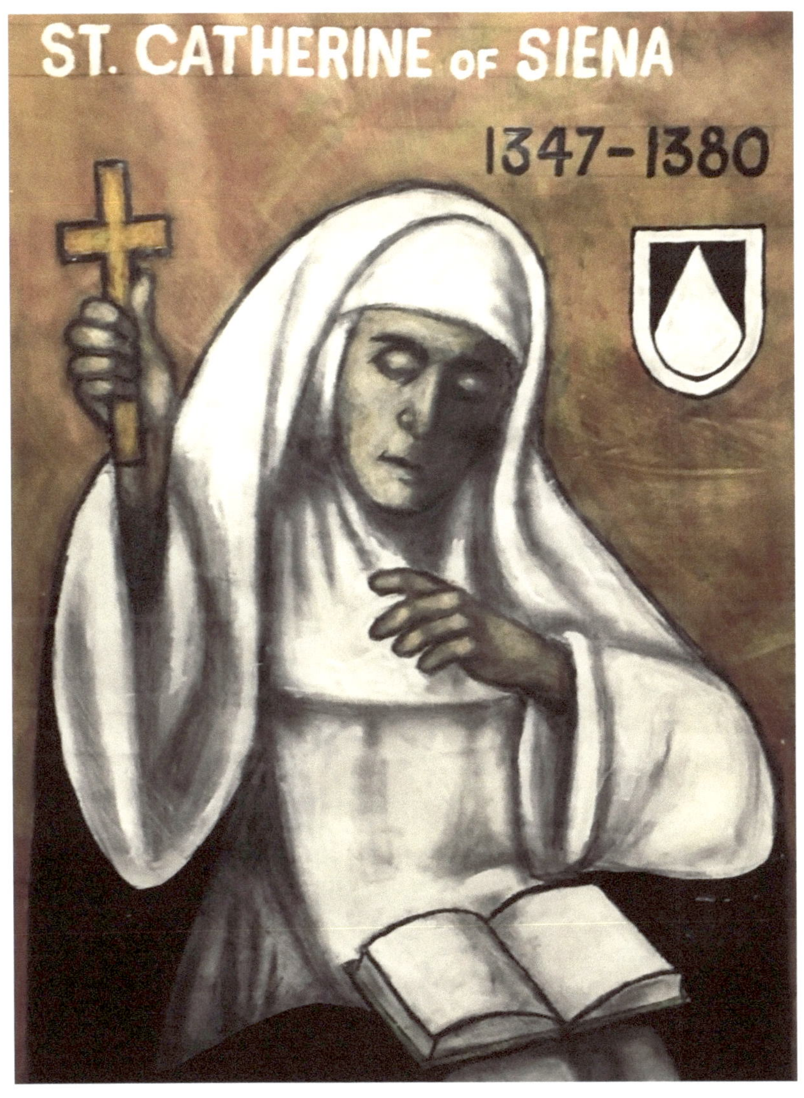
ST. CATHERINE OF SIENA
1347-1380

Saint Antoninus of Florence

'Whoever imagines himself without defect has an excess of pride. God alone is perfect.'

Born in 1389 and baptized as Antonio Pierozzi, Saint Antoninus was an Italian Dominican friar who became Archbishop of Florence. Antoninus entered the Dominican order in 1405 after demonstrating immense zeal and aptitude by learning the canonical law. From a young age he was given various administrative duties within the Order, at which he excelled. In 1436, with the financial assistance of the wealthy Cosimo de Medici, he founded the San Marco convent where Fra Angelico produced much of his famous art. Antoninus also contributed significantly to moral theology with his writing of 'Summa moralis'.

Contrary to his own wishes, in 1446 Antoninus was made Archbishop of Florence after coming under the notice of Pope Eugene IV, who was impressed with his participation in and contribution to the major Church councils of the period.

Antoninus began a society to assist the poor and he personally showed continuing care for them. In the mid-1400s, plague and earthquakes had devastated Florence, but Antoninus won the love and esteem of the people with his remarkable charity and aid given them through this time. In spite of his exalted status in the Church, and his close ties to the Medici regime, who he sometimes served as ambassador to the Holy See, Antoninus maintained an extremely simple way of life as he followed the Dominican Rule.

Saint Antoninus died in 1459 and was canonized in 1523. His feast day is 10 May.

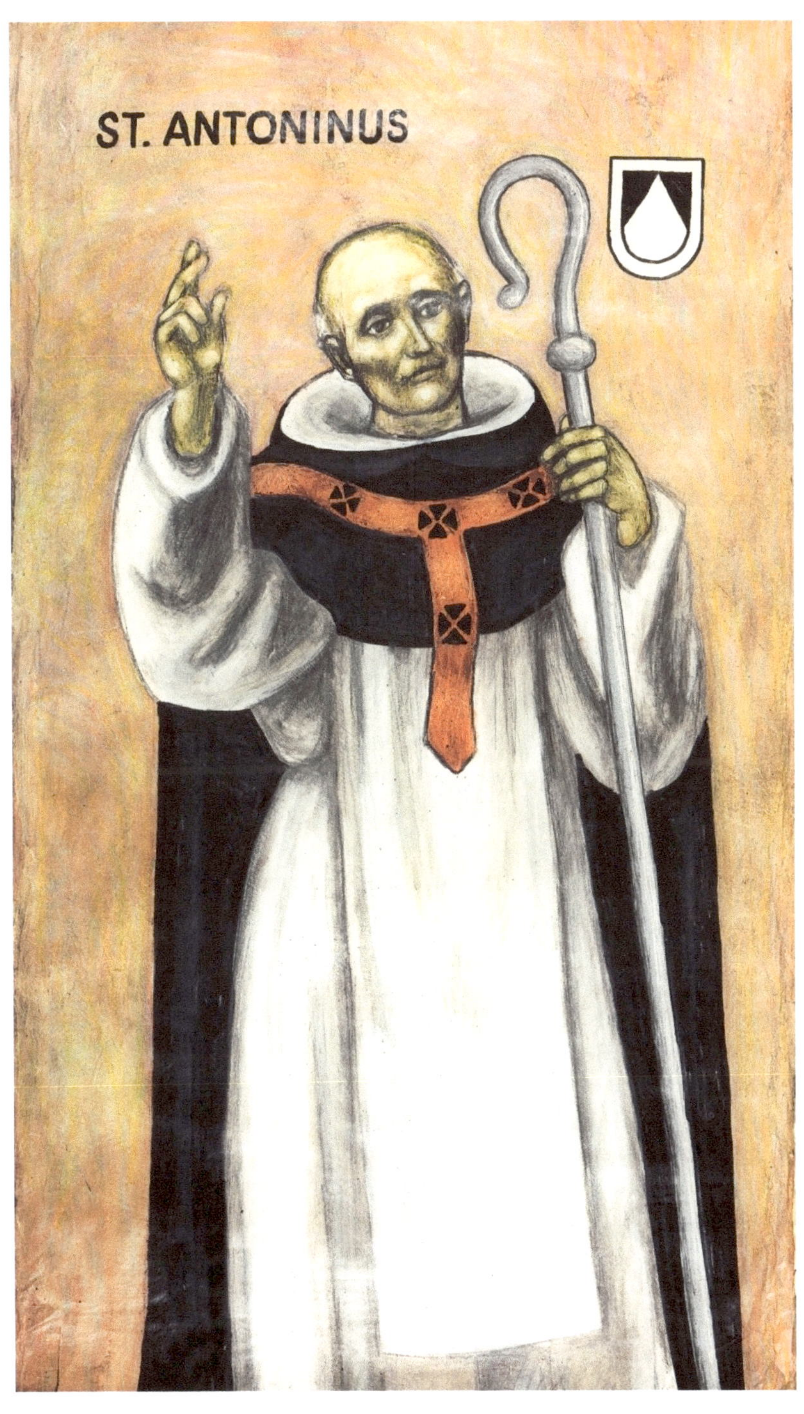
ST. ANTONINUS

Pope Saint Pius V

'O Lord, increase my sufferings and my patience!'

Pope Saint Pius V was born in 1504 in Bosco, Northern Italy as Antonio Ghislieri. He entered the Dominican Order at fourteen years of age and took the name of Michael. He was ordained in 1528 and taught philosophy and theology for sixteen years before acting as prior in Dominican houses where he showed his regard for discipline.

He was appointed Inquisitor at Como and then became Bishop, Cardinal and, in 1558, Principal Inquisitor. He maintained orthodoxy firmly, prosecuting eight French bishops for heresy, and he also opposed nepotism within the church hierarchy.

When elected to be Pope in 1566, in accordance with the Dominican tradition, he immediately reduced the costs of the papal court. Protestantism had attained widespread influence in Europe; and as Pope, he sought to halt its growth and continue combatting other heretical doctrines. He therefore established the 'Congregation of the Index' (which assessed the fitness of literary works for Catholic readership), and he maintained the Inquisition. To overcome the threat of the Ottoman Turks, he organized an alliance between Venice and Spain. The Turks were defeated in the resultant 'Battle of Lepanto', and the Feast of Our Lady of Victories acknowledges her role in response to intercessory prayer throughout Catholic Europe.

Pope Saint Pius also worked to firmly establish the practice of the Council of Trent decrees. He had them published and distributed to all Catholic countries, and required that they were followed. He published the Roman Catechism and standardized the Holy Mass to a form maintained for four hundred years and which is still practised today. He was canonized in 1712.

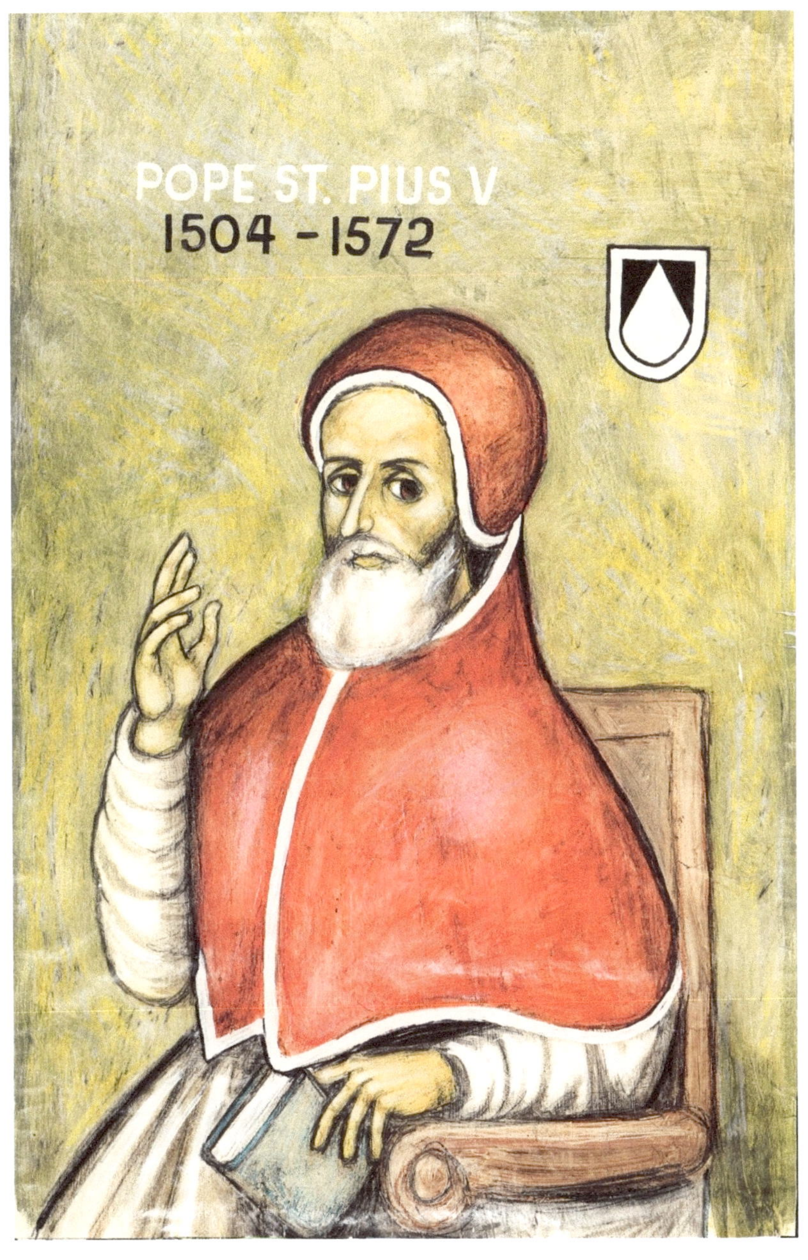
POPE ST. PIUS V
1504 - 1572

Saint Martin de Porres

'Compassion, my dear brothers is preferable to cleanliness.'

Martin was born in Lima, Peru in 1579, the illegitimate son of a Spaniard and a freed slave. When his sister was born in 1581, his father abandoned the family, and his mother supported the family by laundering. He gained some medical knowledge by spending time with a barber/surgeon. He was later accepted into the Dominican Priory of the Holy Rosary in Lima as a volunteer who performed menial tasks and lived with the religious community. Although there was a law against admitting those of African and American Indian ancestry to full membership in religious orders, he was admitted as a Dominican tertiary and then as a lay brother. He rose from servant to almoner, begging significant amounts from the rich to give to the poor, and later laboured in the infirmary.

He undertook severe fasts, prayed and meditated much, was deeply devoted to the Blessed Sacrament, and in his humility asked to be sold into slavery to assist the convent's financial state. He established an orphanage and a hospital for poor children. Martin showed admirable patience and remarkable charity and compassion for the sick, even when contagion seemed a great risk. When there was an epidemic and the novices were separated from the professed by locked doors, Martin was known on several occasions to appear in the locked areas to minister to the sick. Other miraculous occurrences included instantaneous healings, levitation and bilocation. He died in 1639, and was canonised in 1962.

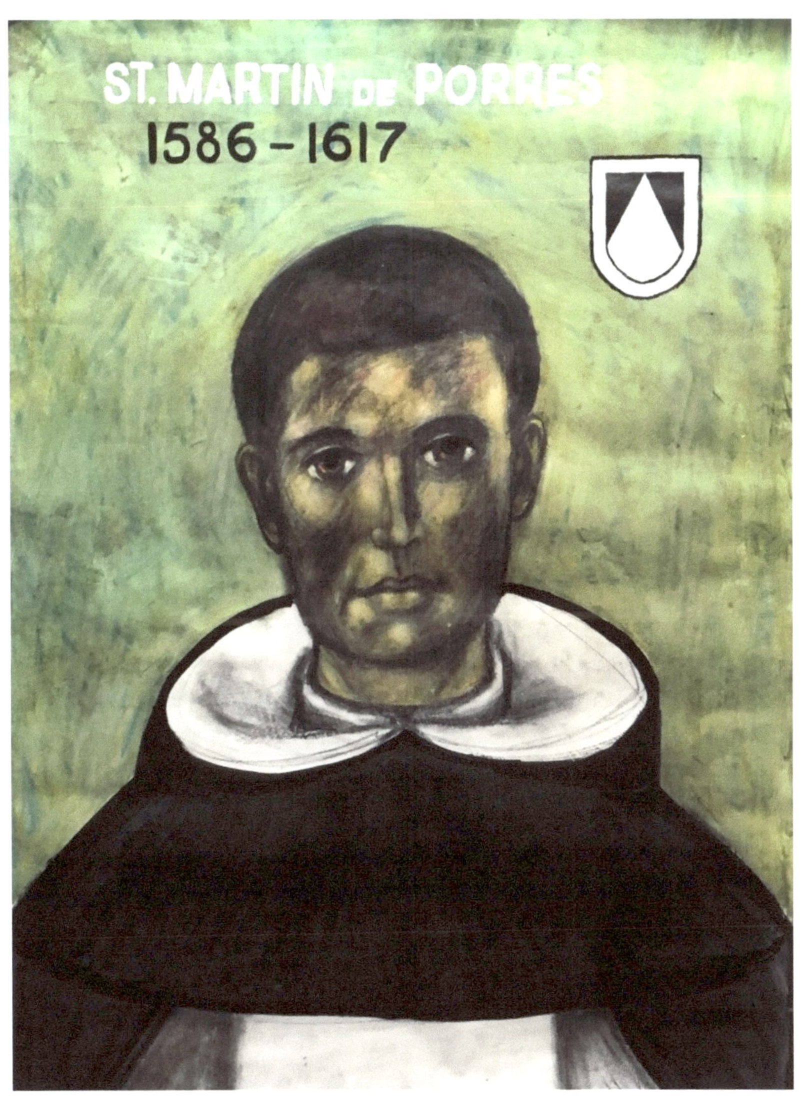
ST. MARTIN DE PORRES
1586 - 1617

Saint Rose of Lima

'Apart from the cross, there is no other ladder by which we may get to heaven.'

Rose was born in Lima, Peru in 1586, and early showed an exceptional reverence and devotion to Jesus and to his mother, Mary. Rose apparently modelled herself on St Catherine of Siena, fasting thrice weekly and undertaking severe penances secretly. She cut off her hair and applied pepper to her face to lessen her attractiveness. She made a vow of virginity, and would have become a nun had her father not forbidden it; so instead she became a Dominican Tertiary (Lay Dominican.)

Rose was an advocate for the oppressed, helped the sick and poor, and worked at handiwork to support the family household. She spent much time before the Blessed Sacrament which she received daily, although this was most uncommon at that time. She began to fast frequently, abstain from meat entirely and then to eat only unappealing food and in quantities just sufficient to sustain life. She wore a metal chain around her waist and a crown with spikes turned downwards. She also slept only two hours nightly on a bed of thorns, stones, broken glass and pottery shards. She offered these mortifications for conversion of sinners, souls in purgatory and as expiation for sin. Throughout these years of severe mortification, Jesus revealed himself to her, and she was sometimes in ecstasy for hours. She died in 1617, and was canonised in 1671. Many miracles have been attributed to her.

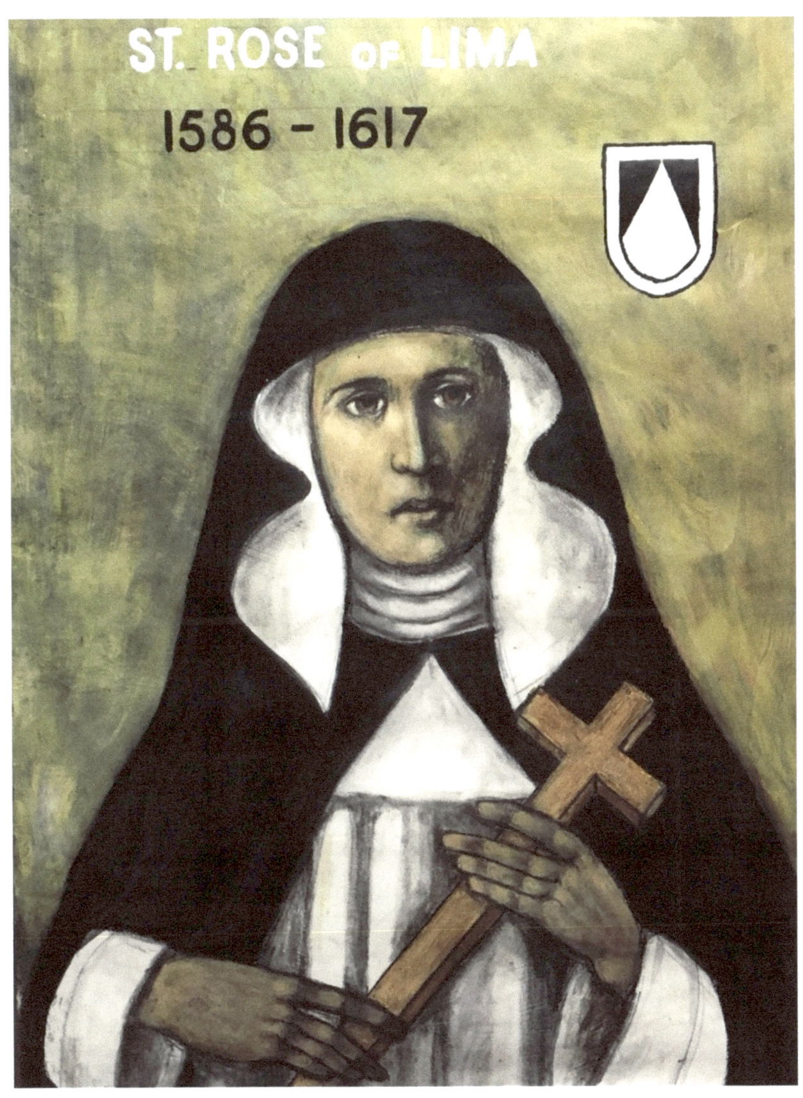
ST. ROSE OF LIMA
1586 - 1617

Saint Lorenzo Ruiz

'I shall die for God and for him I will give many thousands of lives if I had them. Do with me as you please.'

Lorenzo was born in about 1600 in Binondo, Manila, of a Chinese father and Filipino mother. He was educated by the Dominican friars, and joined the Confraternity of the Most Holy Rosary. He married and led a peaceful religious life until one day in 1636, while working as a clerk for the church of Binondo, he was falsely accused of killing a Spaniard. He then sought asylum aboard a ship to Okinawa with three Dominican priests and two others.

Unfortunately, by the time they arrived in Japan, the Tokugawa Shogunate was persecuting Christians. Lorenzo and his companions were imprisoned for over a year and then transferred to Nagasaki where Lorenzo was tortured by being hung upside down over a pit. One hand remained free so that he could signal a denial of his faith, and so be released. Far from denying his faith, however, Lorenzo died from blood loss and suffocation after stating 'I am a Catholic and wholeheartedly do accept death for God. Had I a thousand lives, all these to Him shall I offer'.

He was beatified by Pope John Paul II in 1981 in a ceremony said to be the first beatification outside Rome. In 1987, Lorenzo became the first Filipino to be canonised. A miracle supporting the canonization was the cure of a two-year-old girl whose illness had been diagnosed soon after birth and who had suffered brain atrophy.

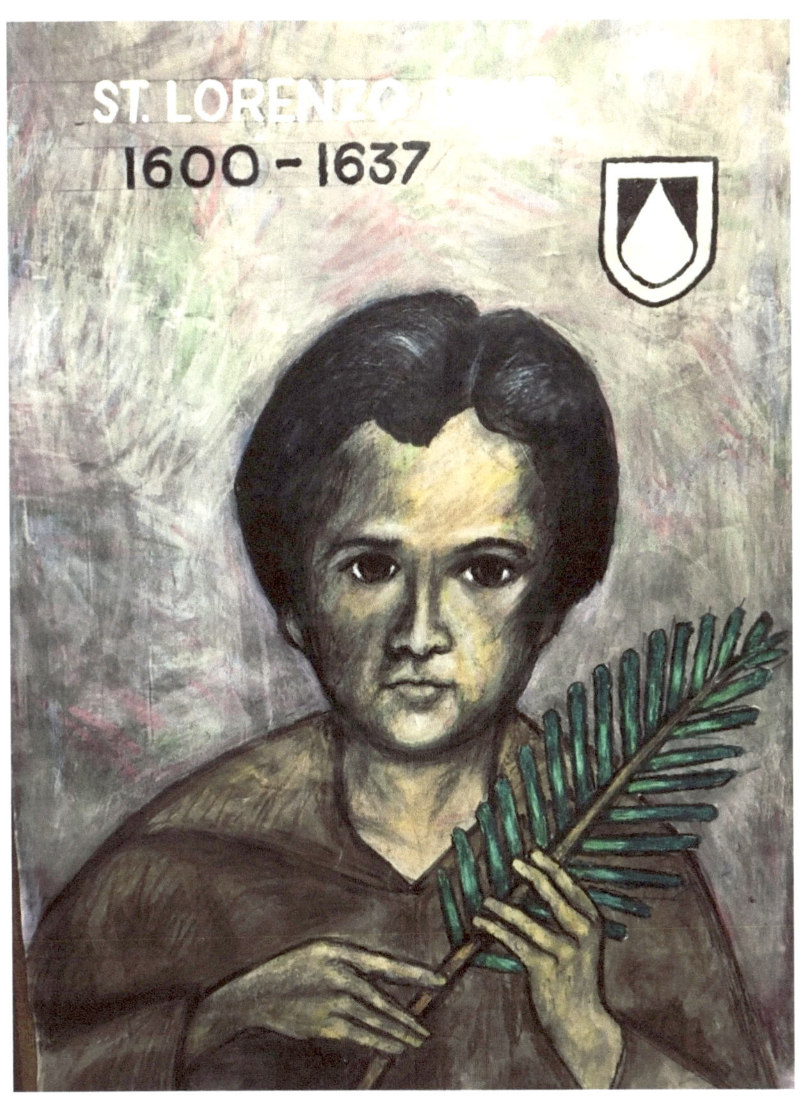
ST. LORENZO
1600 - 1637

Blessed Julia Rodzinska

Blessed Julia was born and christened Stanislawa Marta Jozefa, in 1899 in Nawojowa, Poland. Orphaned before her eleventh birthday, the Dominican Convent took care of her.

On finishing school Stanislawa began training to be a teacher but left to begin her religious formation. She was professed on 3 August 1917 taking the name Maria Julia. Sister Julia later graduated and completed Advanced Studies in Teaching. When only twenty-seven years old, she was appointed Director of a State Primary School in Vilnius. In spite of chronic poor health Sister Julia continued to teach children in secret during World War II. She was arrested by the Gestapo in 1943.

After being kept for a year in isolation, Sister Julia was transported to a disciplinary camp in Prowieniszki. From there she was transferred to the KL Stutthof concentration camp. Arriving on 9th July 1944, she was given the number 40992 and assigned to block No 27 in the 'Jewish Camp'. The conditions were appalling—filth, vermin, overcrowding, absolute lack of privacy and inhumane treatment by criminals and SS soldiers.

In November 1944 as a result of a typhus epidemic the 'Jewish Camp" was isolated and avoided by the authorities. Sister Julia cared for the women of 'death block XXX'. She organized water, dressings and the medicines that were available. She continued to serve even when she finally became infected and was seriously ill. Sister Julia Rodzinska died on the 20th February 1945.

Eva Hoff, a German Jew and fellow prisoner of KL Stutthof, who settled in Sweden, has given an oral and written account of the life and death of Sister Julia in KL Stutthof. This account has been confirmed by other prisoners of KL Stutthof and by Reverend Franciszek Grucza who was Sr Julia's confessor.

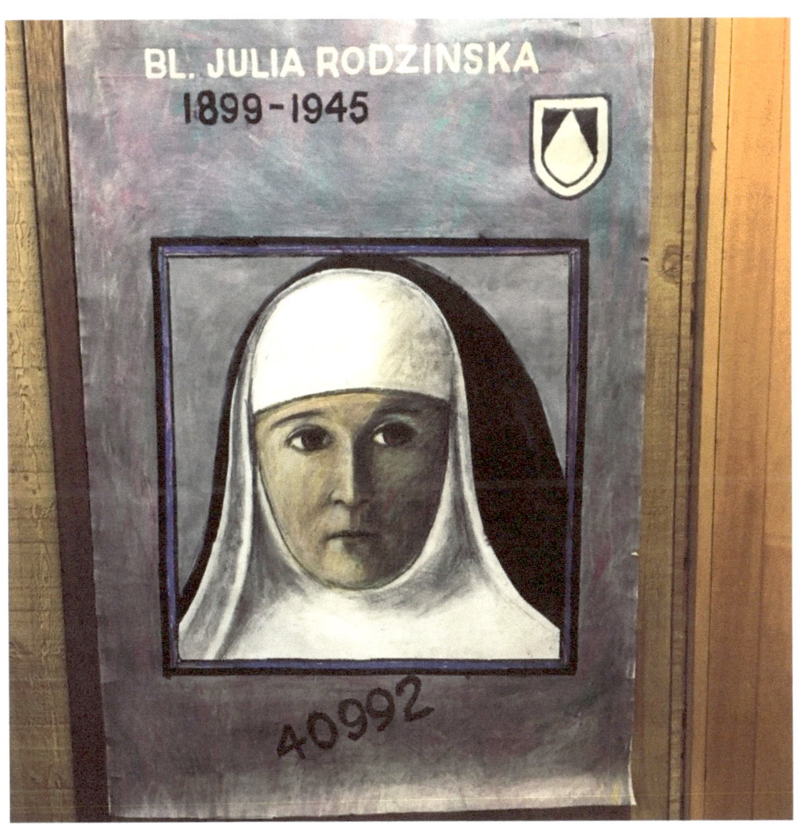
BL. JULIA RODZINSKA
1899-1945
40992

Pier Giorgio Frassati

'All around the sick and all the poor I see a special light which we do not have.'

Young people looking for a role model today need look no further than Blessed Pier Giorgio Frassati who was born in Turin in 1901. He was a young outdoorsman, a political activist, social justice advocate and a Lay Dominican. After World War I, he joined the St Vincent de Paul Society and served the sick and needy, such as disabled returned soldiers and orphaned children.

As a member of 'Catholic Action', he demonstrated against fascism and opposed political violence. He also joined a political party dedicated to promoting the Church's social teaching, particularly the encyclical *Rerum Novarum*. He is often quoted as saying, "Charity is not enough; we need social reform".

Pier Giorgio was fond of sports and had a deep love of nature, especially the mountains. He would organise hiking trips with friends together with a priest so they could have Mass. He was free in sharing his faith with his many friends.

His various social, recreational, political and almsgiving activities were sustained with a deep spiritual life. He devotedly received communion daily and also said the rosary daily.

In 1925, at the age of twenty-four, Pier Giorgio contracted polio and died. Even on his deathbed, he showed his sincere and practical concern for the plight of those he had been helping. He had personally helped many poor people during his short life, and his funeral was marked by thousands of mourners who lined the city streets as the procession passed by.

Pier Giorgio was beatified in 1990 by Pope John Paul II and his feast day is 4 July.

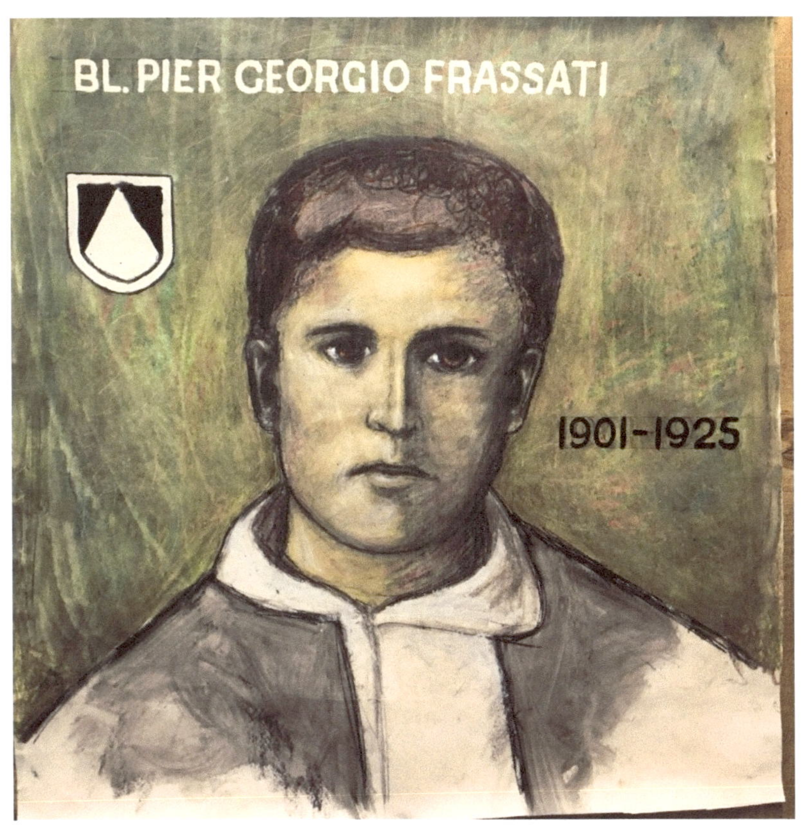
BL. PIER GEORGIO FRASSATI
1901-1925

Dominican Saints' Words

QUOTES FROM DOMINICAN SAINTS

St. Dominic de Guzman: *'We are meant to sow the seed. Not hoard it.' Saint Dominic. (n.d.). AZQuotes.com. Retrieved March 14, 2017, from AZQuotes.com Web site: http://www.azquotes.com/author/41776-Saint_Dominic*

Fra Angelico: *'He who wishes to paint Christ's story must live with Christ.' Fra Angelico. (n.d.). AZQuotes.com. Retrieved March 14, 2017, from AZQuotes.com Web site: http://www.azquotes.com/author/37000-Fra_Angelico*

Jean-Baptiste Henri Lacordaire: *'Nothing is achieved without solitude.' Jean-Baptiste Henri Lacordaire. (n.d.). AZQuotes.com. Retrieved March 14, 2017, from AZQuotes.com Web site: http://www.azquotes.com/quote/1169067*

Pier Frassatti: *'All around the sick and all the poor I see a special light which we do not have.' Saint of the Issue: Blessed Pier Giorgio Frassati - The Torch BC*
https://www.thetorchbc.com/2014/01/.../saint-of-the-issue-blessed-pier-giogio-frassati/

Pope St. Pius V: *'O Lord, increase my sufferings and my patience!' MENDHAM, Life and Pontificate of St. Pius V (London, 1832 and 1835); Acta SS., I May; TOURON, Hommes illustres de l'ordre de St.-Dominique, IV; FALLOUX, Histoire de S. Pie V (Paris, 1853); PASTOR, Gesch. der Papste, ARTAUD DE MONTOR, History of the Popes (New York, 1867); Pope Pius V, the Father of Christendom in Dublin Review, LIX (London, 1866), 273.*

St. Albert the Great. *'If we possess charity then we possess God for God is Charity.' catholicsaints.info/saint-albert-the-great/*

St. Antonius of Florence: *'Whoever imagines himself without defect has an excess of pride. God alone is perfect.' www.loyalbooks.com/.../text/Thoughts-and-Counsels-of-the-Saints-for-Every-Day.txt*

St. Catherine of Siena: *'Be who God meant you to be and you will set the world on fire.' St Catherine of Siena. (n.d.). AZQuotes.com. Retrieved March 14, 2017, from AZQuotes.com Web site: http://www.azquotes.com/author/17881-St_Catherine_of_Siena*

St. Lorenzo Ruiz: *'I shall die for God and for Him I will give many thousands of lives if I had them. Do with me as you please.' faithofthefatherssaintquote.blogspot.com/.../saint-quote-saint-lorenzo-ruiz-of-manila.h...*

St. Margaret of Hungary: *'I prefer to be among those who consider that they have no time to lose if they wish to give God all the glory that they can before they die.' The Big Book Of Women Saints | Harper Collins Australia*
www.harpercollins.com.au/9780060825126/

St. Martin de Porres: *'Compassion, my dear brothers is preferable to cleanliness.' sanctoral.com/en/saints/saint_martin_de_porres.html*

St. Rose of Lima: *'Apart from the cross, there is no other ladder by which we may get to heaven.' Rose of Lima. (n.d.). AZQuotes.com. Retrieved March 14, 2017, from AZQuotes.com Web site: http://www.azquotes.com/author/21545-Rose_of_Lima*

St. Thomas Aquinas: *'To one who has faith no explanation is necessary. To one without faith no explanation is possible' 59 Thomas Aquinas Quotes | ChristianQuotes.info*
https://www.christianquotes.info/quotes-by-author/thomas-aquinas-quotes/

Blessed Margaret of Castello:*'Oh, if only you knew what I carried in my heart, you would marvel!' catholicism.org/blessed-margaret-castello.html*

St. Peter of Verona: *'God loves us beyond comprehension and we cannot diminish God's love for us.' Saint Peter. (n.d.). AZQuotes.com. Retrieved March 15, 2017, from AZQuotes.com Web site: http://www.azquotes.com/author/39163-Saint_Peter*

St. Hyacinth of Poland: *'For [poverty]is the testament or authentic instrument by which we claim eternal life.'*

From the bull of his canonization by Clement VIII. published by Fontanini, in 1729, in Codice Canonization; his life by Alberti, and the Polish historians. See Touron, de Vic S. Domin. l. 6, et Cuper the Bollandist, t. 3, Aug. p. 309.

Bibliography

Albertus Magnus. (17 Feb 2017). In *Wikipedia.* Retrieved 21 March 2017 from https://en.wikipedia.org/wiki/Albertus_Magnus

Biography of St Margaret of Hungary. Solemn Charge. Retrieved 21` March 2017 from http://www.solemncharge.com/SaintOfTheDay.aspx?key=St-Margaret-of-Hungary

Blessed Dominican Sister-Julia Rodzinska. (19th Feb 2013). Stutthof Museum Notes. Retrieved 21 March 2017 from https://www.facebook.com/notes/muzeum-stutthofstutthof-museum/blessed-dominican-sister-julia-rodzi%C5%84ska483455971711442/

Blessed Margaret of Castello. (2011). Roman Catholic Saints. Retrieved 21 March 2017 from http://www.roman-catholic-saints.com/blessed-margaret-of-castello.html

Blessed Pier Giorgio Frassati. Lay Fraternities of St. Dominic- Province of St Joseph. Retrieved 20 March 2017 from http://laydominicans.org/study/dominican-saints/blessed-pier-giorgio-frassati/

Brady, G.K. (1957). *Saint Dominic Pilgrim of Light.* London. Burns and Oates

Bullough, S. (2008). Saint Dominic Spanish Priest, In *Encyclopaedia Britannica.* Retrieved 20 March 2017 from https://www.britannica.com/biography/Saint-Dominic

Catherine of Sienna. (17 March 2017). In *Wikipedia*, Retrieved 20 March 2017 from https://en.wikipedia.org/wiki/Catherine_of_Siena

Congar, Y. (1968). *St Thomas Aquinas: Servant of Truth.* Dominican Publication of article by same name, first printed in "Faith and Spiritual Life" trans A. Manson and L.C. Sheppard. New York. Herder

Dominican Saints 101: St. Peter Martyr. (3 June 2012). Dominican Friars Province of St. Joseph. Retrieved 22 March 2017 from https://opeast.org/2012/06/dominican-saints-101-st-peter-martyr/

Gardner, E. (1908). St Catherine of Siena. In *The Catholic Encyclopedia,* New York, Appleton. Retrieved 20 March 2017 from New Advent: http://www.newadvent.org/cathen/03447a.htm

History Of The Order. The Dominican Friars-England and Scotland. Retrieved 20 March 2017 from http://english.op.org/about-us/dominican-order/history-of-the-order.htm

Hyacinth of Poland. (8 Oct 2016). In *Wikipedia.* Retrieved 22 March 2017 from https://en.wikipedia.org/wiki/Hyacinth_of_Poland

Jordan of Saxony. (28 Jan2017). In *Wikipedia.* Retrieved 21 March 2017 from https://en.wikipedia.org/wiki/Jordan_of_Saxony

Lorenzo Ruiz. (19 Feb 2017). In *Wikipedia.* Retrieved 22 March 2017 from https://en.wikipedia.org/wiki/Lorenzo_Ruiz

Martin de Porres. (18 March 2017). In *Wikipedia.* Retrieved 22 March 2017 from https://en.wikipedia.org/wiki/Martin_de_Porres

McMahon, A. (1907). St Antoninus. In *The Catholic Encyclopedia,* New York, Appleton. Retrieved 18 March 2017, from New Advent: http://www.newadvent.org/cathen/01585b.htm

New Catholic Encyclopedia. Palatine U.S.A., Heraty, 1981

O'Connor, J.B., (1916). *Saint Dominic and the Order of Preachers.* New York, Holy Name Bureau. Retrieved electronically 20 March 2017 from Jacques Maritain Center, https://www3.nd.edu/~maritain/jmc/etext/dominic.htm

Peter of Verona. (21 Feb 2017). In *Wikipedia.* Retrieved 22 March 2017 from https://en.wikipedia.org/wiki/Peter_of_Verona

Pier Giorgio Frassati. (15 March 2017). In *Wikipedia.* Retrieved 20 March 2017 from https://en.wikipedia.org/wiki/Pier_Giorgio_Frassati

Pope Pius V. (6 March 2017). In *Wikipedia*. Retrieved 21 March 2017 from https://en.wikipedia.org/wiki/Pope_Pius_V

Raymond of Penyafort. (16 January 2017). In *Wikipedia.* Retrieved 20 March 2017 from https://en.wikipedia.org/wiki/Raymond_of_Penyafort

Resurrection Miracles - Bl Margaret of Castello, The Blind and Crippled Wonder-Worker, A.D. 1287 - 13th April A.D. 1320. Jeevan Jal Ministries. Retrieved 21 March 2017 from http://www.jeevanjal.org/jeevanjal/rm11.html

Rodriguez, D. (5 May 2016). *Pope St. Pius V- May 5.* St Vincent Ferrer Foundation of Texas. Accessed 21 March 2017 at http://svfonline.org/pope-st-pius-v-may-5/

Rose of Lima. (16 March 2017). In *Wikipedia.* Retrieved 22 March 2017 from https://en.wikipedia.org /wiki/Rose_of_Lima

Saint Antoninus Archbishop of Florence. (2009). *Encyclopaedia Britannica.* Accessed 18 March 2007from https://www.britannica.com/biography/Saint-Antoninus

Saint Dominic. The Dominican Sisters of Saint Cecilia. Retrieved 20 March 2017 from http://www.nashvilledominican.org/our-vowed-life/st-dominic/

Saint Hyacinth Missionary Preacher and Thaumaturge (1894). In J.G. Shea (ed.), *Little Pictorial Lives of the Saints*, New York, Benziger. Retrieved electronically from Magnificat website on 22 March 2017 at http://sanctoral.com/en/saints/saint_hyacinth.html

St Lorenzo Ruiz. (n.d.) stjohnleesburg.org. Retrieved 22 March 2017 from http://www.stjohnleesburg.org/bp/Saints/St_Lorenzo_Ruiz_profile.pdf

St Martin de Porres. (6 January 2016). Legion of Mary. Retrieved 22 March 2017 from https://www.motheroflightcenter.com/st-martin-de-porres

St. Rose of Lima Peruvian Saint. (10 March 2016). In *Encyclopaedia Britannica*. Retrieved 22 March 2017 from https://www.britannica.com/biography/Saint-Rose-of-Lima

The Miracles of Saint Dominic. (23 August 2012). Dominican Central Province. Retrieved 20 March 2017 from http://opcentral.org/blog/the-miracles-of-saint-dominic/

Thomas Aquinas. (17 March 2017). In *Wikipedia*. Retrieved 21 March 2017 from https://en.wikipedia/wiki/Thomas_Aquinas

Biographies' Editors

Blessed Jordan of Saxony	Louise Simento
Blessed Julia Rodzinska	Louise Simento
Blessed Margaret of Castello	Salvina Kelly
Blessed Pier Giorgio Frassati	David Porter
Saint Albert the Great	Louise Simento
Saint Antoninus of Florence	David Porter
Saint Catherine of Siena	David Porter
Saint Dominic de Guzman	Salvina Kelly
Saint Hyacinth	Philip Martin
Saint Lorenzo Ruiz	Philip Martin
Saint Margaret of Hungary	Salvina Kelly
Saint Martin de Porres	Philip Martin
Saint Peter Martyr (Peter of Verona)	Philip Martin
Saint Raymond of Penyafort	David Porter
Saint Rose of Lima	Philip Martin
Saint Thomas Aquinas	Louise Simento

Lightning Source UK Ltd.
Milton Keynes UK
UKHW050711080322
399723UK00001B/29